6:16
Lexile: _____

AR/BL: _____0.9_____

AR Points: _____0.5_____

My Pet

My Cat

By Cate Foley

Children's Press
A Division of Grolier Publishing
New York / London / Hong Kong / Sydney
Danbury, Connecticut

Photo Credits: Cover, pp. 5, 7, 9, 11, 13, 15, 17, 19, 21 by Maura Boruchow
Contributing Editor: Jeri Cipriano
Book Design: Nelson Sa

Visit Children's Press on the Internet at:
http://publishing.grolier.com

Library of Congress Cataloging-in-Publication Data

Foley, Cate.
My cat / by Cate Foley.
p. cm.—(My pet)
Includes bibliographical references and index.
ISBN 0-516-23183-9 (lib. bdg.)—ISBN 0-516-23286-X (pbk.)
1. Cats—Miscellaneous—Juvenile literature. [1. Cats. 2. Pets.] I. Title. II. My pet (Children's Press)

SF445.7 .F65 2000
636.8—dc21

00-060218

Contents

I am Tom.

This is my cat, Tabby.

5

Tabby and I are best friends.

7

How does Tabby say hello?

He rubs my leg to say hello.

How does Tabby play?

He **pounces** on the string when he plays.

10

11

How does Tabby tell
me he is hungry?

Tabby **meows** when
he is hungry.

13

What does Tabby eat?

Tabby eats cat food.

I also give him water
to drink.

How does Tabby stay clean?

He licks his fur to stay clean.

17

How do I know when
Tabby feels good?

Tabby **purrs** when he
feels good.

He purrs when I pet him.

19

What do I like best about Tabby?

He keeps me company – even when I sleep!

New Words

meows (mee-**owz**) makes
   a sound that cats make
pounces (**powns**-ez)
   jumps on
purrs (**perz**) the soft
   sounds a cat makes
   when it feels good

To Find Out More

Books
Barn Cat: A Counting Book
by Carol P. Saul
Little, Brown & Company

Milton
by Haydé Ardalan
Chronicle Books

Web Sites
Cat of the Day
http://www.catoftheday.com/
See pictures of cats and find out more about them. You can send in a picture of your cat to be Pet of the Day.

The Cat Club
http://www.catclub.net/
Learn about different kinds of cats and how to take care of a cat. You can join the cat club and chat with other cat lovers!

Index

About the Author
Cate Foley writes and edits books for children. She lives in New Jersey with her husband and son.

Reading Consultants
Kris Flynn, Coordinator, Small School District Literacy, The San Diego County Office of Education

Shelly Forys, Certified Reading Recovery Specialist, W.J. Zahnow Elementary School, Waterloo, IL

Peggy McNamara, Professor, Bank Street College of Education, Reading and Literacy Program